BURIED IN GARBAGE

Bobbie Kalman & Janine Schaub

The Crabtree Environment Series

CRABTREE PUBLISHING COMPANY

Created by Bobbie Kalman

For my best friend Magdalena

Writing team
Bobbie Kalman
Janine Schaub

Editors
Claudia Forgas
Peter Crabtree

Computer Layout
Suzanne Jensen

Mechanicals
David Willis
Diane Coderre

Color Separations
Systems Color

Printer
Lake Book Manufacturing

A very special thanks to the teachers and students of Hoover Elementary School, Samantha Crabtree, Sarah Giesbrecht, Barney Bajardi, Claudia Forgas, Suzanne Jensen, and Kirsten Jensen.

Published by
Crabtree Publishing Company

1110 Kamato Road	350 Fifth Avenue	73 Lime Walk
Unit 4	Suite 3308	Headington
Mississauga, Ontario	New York	Oxford OX3 7AD
Canada L4W 2P3	N.Y. 10118	United Kingdom

Cataloguing in Publication Data

Kalman, Bobbie, 1947-
  Buried in garbage

(The Crabtree environment series)
Includes index.
ISBN 0-86505-424-X (bound) ISBN 0-86505-454-1 (pbk.)

1. Refuse and refuse disposal - Juvenile literature.
2. Refuse disposal facilities - Juvenile literature.
I. Title. II. Series: Kalman, Bobbie, 1947- .
The Crabtree environment series.

TD792.K35 1991   j 363.72'8

Contents

It's your garbage!

You have just finished your lunch. On your way out of the classroom, you toss your garbage into the trash can. Your drink box, sandwich wrapping, apple core, yogurt cup, and paper bag are only a small part of the waste that you will throw away today—and that is not all the garbage that is yours. Every day your local government produces waste as it provides services for you and your family. Schools and recreation centers are examples of services that you use. Businesses and industry produce more waste while making goods for you to buy. Along with the waste you yourself produce, extra garbage is created by these other sources. Indirectly this is also your garbage!

Not only do you create garbage at home, you discard many things at school, too.

Types of waste

Your community disposes of many different kinds of waste: some of it comes in the form of gas, some liquid, and some solid. Sewage is an example of **liquid waste**, and car exhaust is an example of **gaseous waste**. All these kinds of wastes pollute the environment in which we live. In this book we talk about **solid waste**—the waste we commonly call trash, rubbish, or garbage.

Garbage can be a combination of paper, food, glass, metal, plastic, textiles, and wood. It includes waste from offices, schools, construction sites, farms, and industries as well as waste from your home.

A community creates many types of waste each day: liquid, gaseous, and solid waste, called garbage.

What is garbage?

Each family in your town or city produces between forty-five and a hundred pounds (twenty and forty-five kilograms) of trash every week. What is all this garbage?

Food and garden waste Vegetable peels, fruit skins and cores, leftovers, garden clippings, and leaves make up about one third of our garbage. It is hard to believe, but almost one quarter of the food we buy ends up being thrown out.

Paper and paper products Another third of our garbage is made up of paper and paper products. This portion contains newspapers, mail, and old telephone directories. A lot of it also comes from empty boxes and other packaging material.

Glass, plastic, metal The last third of our garbage includes various items made out of glass, metal, and plastic, such as jars, cans, and bottles.

food and garden (30%)	glass (10%)
paper and cardboard (30%)	metal (10%)
miscellaneous (12%) (rubber, textiles, plastic mixed with other materials)	plastic (8%)

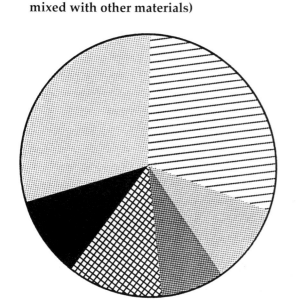

Buried in garbage!

When you throw something "away," it does not disappear. When you drop a soda can on the ground and walk away, you may not see it anymore, but every piece of trash that you throw out must end up somewhere!

Until recently we have not thought much about garbage. We threw away anything we no longer wanted. The world is now feeling the results of our thoughtless actions. We have too much garbage, and we are running out of places to put it. We cannot ignore garbage any longer. Governments must pass stricter laws to control waste; businesses must cut down on the waste they produce. Each man, woman, and child needs to get involved in reducing his or her waste. Garbage must be the concern of every person each and every day because, if we continue producing it at this rate, we will soon be buried in our own garbage!

From natural resources to trash

When you think of garbage, you probably imagine a pile of used-up, good-for-nothing junk. Yet garbage is far from useless. All the items that make up our garbage were once part of the natural world. We call these things **natural resources** because people use these raw materials for food, shelter, fuel, and clothing. Air, sunshine, water, animals, plants, and trees are some examples. Stone, sand, and minerals such as iron ore and gold are also natural resources. Some resources such as coal and oil are called **non-renewable resources** because they take millions of years to form and there is only a limited supply available.

Paper, glass, and cans

Many resources are **processed**, or made into other forms, before we use them. For instance, ground-up wood, called pulp, is used to make paper. Glass is made from a mixture of white sand, soda, and lime, which is melted at extremely hot temperatures. All the cans found in household garbage are made from various metals such as iron, tin, and bauxite.

Plastic—strong and durable

Plastic is a modern invention that has changed our world. It is strong and durable, yet it can be molded into any shape. It can also withstand extreme temperatures. Plastic is made from **petroleum**, one of our non-renewable resources. Petroleum is another word for unrefined oil, a thick black liquid found inside the earth. Countless things are made of plastic. Here are just a few items: bottles, caps, food containers, tool handles, plugs, switches, telephones, computer equipment, toys, shoes, furniture, and film. If you look around, you will see that we are, indeed, living in the age of plastic!

Long-lasting garbage

Plastic lasts a long time and can resist wear and tear. It is dangerous to the natural world because the most poisonous wastes that threaten the earth are created during its production.

Plastic is hard to dispose of because it will not break down. Some plastics take hundreds and even thousands of years to **disintegrate**, or separate into little pieces. For the same reason, the natural resources in most types of plastic cannot be separated and recycled. Although durability is the best quality of plastic when it is being used, it is its worst quality when plastic becomes a piece of garbage.

Reusing and conserving resources

We have found ways to recycle some of the natural resources found in garbage, but we still have a long way to go. By buying and discarding products such as those made from plastic, we are creating permanent garbage and hazardous waste. But most important of all, we are using up the natural resources of the earth. When these are gone, there will be no way to obtain more. It is up to us to conserve these precious resources while they still exist.

◀*(Opposite; top) Trees are a natural resource. (bottom, left) Plastic is made from oil, a natural resource. (bottom, right) Much of today's garbage does not break down into the ingredients from which it was made. It cannot become part of the earth again.*

The garbage explosion

In the past, bits of rag were used to make rag rugs.

Less than two hundred years ago the word "garbage" was almost unknown. In those days everything was used and reused, and very little was thrown out. Bits of fabric ended up as patchwork quilts and rag rugs, and kitchen scraps were fed to the pigs. Ash from the fire and leftovers of fat were used to make soap. Most people made the articles they needed in their own homes.

Machine-made goods

About one hundred and fifty years ago great changes began taking place in the world. Machines were invented that could produce large numbers of goods easily and cheaply. Suddenly all sorts of new things became available for ordinary people to purchase. Thousands of people moved to the cities to work in the many factories that were built. They no longer made the things they needed in their homes. They started buying factory-made goods.

A sudden growth in population

Not only did people learn how to manufacture many things, they also made new discoveries in medicine. As a result fewer people were dying of diseases, and the population grew very quickly. Today the world supports a huge population of five billion people. Within thirty years, this number is expected to double.

Living in a consumer society

Those of us who live in industrialized countries are part of what is called a **consumer society**. When we need something, we buy it; when we want something, we also buy it. As long as we can afford it, we feel it is our right to purchase whatever we like. When something breaks, wears out, or goes out of fashion, we throw it away. We know that almost everything we own can be replaced relatively easily.

The garbage crisis

The garbage crisis that we are now facing is the result of living in a consumer society. We buy all sorts of things that were once considered unnecessary. Our lives also seem much busier, so we are always trying to save time. We purchase **convenience items** such as frozen dinners and snack packs. We choose to eat foods that come in single-serving cans and boxes. Much of what we buy is disposable, as well. It is meant to be thrown away. The final result is that there are many more people producing much more garbage and there is a lot less space for its disposal.

(Opposite; bottom) Most of the people in the world live in big cities and use factory-made goods. ▶

When new discoveries were made in medicine, the population of the world grew quickly. Since two hundred years ago, it has increased from one to five billion. In thirty years it is expected to double.

Garbage collection

In the past there was no need for someone to collect garbage from small towns and villages. Each family burned its own rubbish or brought it to a public dumping ground just outside a town. In those days garbage did not contain the dangerous chemicals today's garbage contains.

How it began

In cities, however, getting rid of garbage was more of a problem. Many people just threw their refuse out the window. This dangerous practice fed the rat population, spread disease, and created a horrible stink. In some cities garbage collectors drove a horse and cart through the streets and took away people's trash for a fee. Junk collectors also traveled the streets and bought up goods that people no longer needed. They repaired these items and then sold them again.

The garbage wagon

When the garbage wagon came down the street, everyone knew it was there. The clippity-clop of the horses, the call of the driver, and the smell of the garbage signaled its arrival. Huge clouds of buzzing flies and hungry birds followed it as it made its smelly way through the city streets.

Garbage pickup

We no longer hear the calls of the old-fashioned garbage collector. Instead, we have special "garbage days" on which our trash is picked up. On these days everyone brings their garbage cans to the curb in the morning and by evening the cans have been emptied. If you live in a big city, hundreds of garbage trucks are at work. They collect from restaurants, theaters, stores, office and apartment buildings, hotels, parks, schools, and homes.

The modern garbage truck

The modern garbage truck does not smell nearly as much as the old garbage wagon did because the garbage is completely enclosed. Modern garbage trucks are enormous and hold huge amounts of trash. A mechanical arm on the truck squeezes the garbage so it takes up much less space. After the sanitation workers throw the trash into the back, they push a button. The arm comes down, covering the garbage and pushing it into the middle of the truck.

Where does all this garbage go?

Garbage collection is a service provided by the government of your town or city. A large part of your parents' taxes pay for the collection and disposal of garbage. In cities garbage from homes, offices, factories, and schools is taken to **transfer stations**, where it is roughly sorted and compacted to take up less space. Then it is stuffed onto huge **transfer trailers** and brought to a **landfill site** or **incinerator**. In small towns, the garbage is taken directly to the landfill site.

(left) An old-fashioned garbage wagon

Sanitation workers can collect garbage for several hours before they have to dump their load.

Conduct an interview

If you talk to a modern-day garbage collector, you may be surprised to find out what he or she can tell you about your community. Conduct an interview with a local sanitary official. Tape-record the interview and then play it back for your classmates. Have several questions prepared before your meeting. Sample questions might be:

• What kinds of valuable things do people throw away?
• At what time of year do people throw out the most waste?
• How much waste does the average home dispose of each week?
• From which areas is it the most difficult to collect garbage? Why?

City garbage is sorted and compacted at a transfer station. It is then transported to a landfill site.

11

Landfilling

Although some communities still leave their garbage at open-air dumps, this is a very dangerous method of waste disposal. Much of our garbage is poisonous. At a dump site the poisons seep into the ground and contaminate the surrounding environment. Dumps also attract birds, flies, and rats, which can spread disease. Landfilling, a better method of storing garbage, is used by many modern cities.

Leachate seeps through layers of dirt and garbage and can enter the ground water if it is not carefully monitored and collected.

Layers of dirt and garbage

Landfill sites are usually located in old gravel pits or deep valleys. A layer of clay is spread along the bottom and sides of the pit to create a protective liner about five feet (a meter-and-a-half) thick. At the end of each day the waste is covered with soil to cut down on odors and keep away animals. When a landfill site is completely full, it is blanketed with another thick layer of clay and more soil. Sometimes shrubs and trees are planted on top. Old landfills become parks, parking lots, and ski hills.

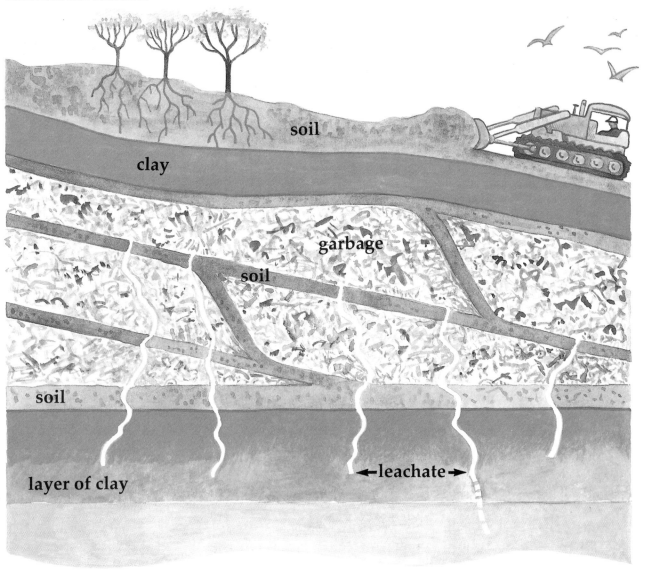

soil

clay

garbage

soil

soil

layer of clay

←leachate→

This photograph shows how leachate can contaminate the surrounding soil and water at a landfill site.

Toxic fumes and leachate

As garbage in the landfill site decomposes, it releases dangerous gases such as **methane** into the air. These gases must be vented safely to prevent fires and explosions. As the garbage breaks down and mixes with rain, it produces **leachate**, a poisonous liquid. Leachate seeps through the rotting trash and can make its way into the ground.

In a landfill site the clay liner at the bottom of the pit prevents most of the leachate from seeping, or leaching, into the soil. The leachate that accumulates must be monitored carefully. It should be collected regularly and taken to toxic-waste facilities so that it will not poison the **ground water**, the water beneath the surface of the earth that many people use as their drinking water.

Careful checking

Landfill sites, no matter how well maintained, are dangerous to the environment. The waste in the site must be checked regularly for many years after the site is covered over. The soil underneath the site must also be tested for contamination because, as garbage continues to break down, it continually forms more leachate.

No more space for garbage

Most people do not want to live near a landfill site because they are worried about leachate and toxic fumes. Few communities allow landfill sites to be started in their areas. As a result many towns and cities are running out of space to dump their garbage. Nearly every landfill site in every major city around the world is now or, will soon be, full. When this space runs out, where will we put our garbage then?

Sandra's trip to a landfill site

Sandra and her dad spent all weekend doing their spring cleaning. On Monday afternoon they loaded a broken bunk bed, Sandra's old bike, and eighteen garbage bags full of junk onto the back of their pickup truck. Sandra had never been to a dump before and was interested in seeing one. Her dad explained that they were going to a special kind of dump called a landfill site.

When Sandra and her dad arrived at the landfill, they joined a long line of trucks waiting to empty their loads. Their small pickup seemed tiny compared to the enormous commercial-waste trucks on the road. Each vehicle drove onto a scale to weigh its garbage.

A smelly, noisy pit

After a lengthy wait Sandra's dad backed up his truck to the **tipping face**. The tipping face is the spot at the edge of a slope where trucks dump their loads. Sandra watched the many bulldozers below move the garbage and compact it. She thought that working in a landfill would be a very noisy and smelly job! Not only was there a constant roar of waste-moving vehicles, the air was also filled with the shrill cries of gulls and hundreds of other hungry birds.

Covering the trash

It was late in the afternoon when Sandra and her dad were finished. As they were leaving, they saw huge bulldozers push earth over the top of the garbage. In the days, weeks, and centuries to follow, the waste below would slowly decompose.

So much garbage!

On the way home, Sandra thought about the many trucks that dumped garbage at the landfill site. She did not realize how much waste was being thrown away in her community each day. She was shocked by the sight of all that garbage! She wondered where garbage would be taken when this site was covered over in a few years.

It felt good to clean the house and get rid of all that junk, but Sandra felt guilty about throwing it all away. Could she and her family have recycled some of it or sold it at a garage sale? Could they have donated the toys and games to a charitable organization? Could she have had her old bike fixed instead of buying a new one?

Time for a change

It was too late to do anything about the trash Sandra and her father just dumped, but Sandra knew that she could do something about their future garbage. How do you think Sandra and her family could change their wasteful ways? Are you putting your suggestions to work with your family?

Add up the garbage

You create two pounds (about one kilogram) of personal waste every day. Business and government create more for every citizen. Altogether, you are responsible for seven pounds (three kilograms) of daily refuse. If you multiply this figure by the population of your city, you can calculate how much waste is thrown away daily in your area. Using the three Rs, how much waste could your city reduce?

Off to the dump!

Suggest a class trip to a landfill site. Be prepared to ask the person who conducts the tour about all aspects of landfilling. Here are some sample questions:

- How thick is the bottom clay liner?
- What tests were done before the site was opened to check its suitability as a landfill?
- Who owns the site? When was it opened? What was the construction cost?
- Who is allowed to bring waste to the site? Is there a user's fee to dump waste?
- Are there any hazardous materials dumped in the landfill? Are there provisions and regulations for dealing with hazardous wastes?
- How much solid waste is disposed of at the site each day?
- How are pests, odors, blowing trash, and leachate controlled?
- Who monitors the site?
- How often is the leachate collected?
- Burning of garbage is not permitted at many landfill sites. Is there any garbage burning at this site?
- Have any problems been reported concerning the health of the people or wildlife in the areas surrounding the landfill?
- How much does it cost to take care of the waste once it is in the landfill?
- How many years is the landfill expected to last?
- After the landfill site is closed, who will take care of it?
- Where will the garbage go after this landfill site is full?

Sandra was shocked when she saw all that garbage! Have you ever visited a landfill?

Incineration

Many communities are running out of landfill space and have built incineration plants to deal with their solid waste. Incineration is the burning of garbage at extremely high temperatures in huge furnaces called incinerators. When waste is incinerated, it is reduced to gas and two kinds of ashes.

Mass-burn incinerators

The most common type of incinerator used in cities is called the **mass-burn incinerator**. Mass-burn incinerators can burn all sorts of garbage. Other types of incinerators are designed to handle only garbage that has been thoroughly sorted at transfer stations.

Ordinary garbage trucks bring their loads directly to a mass-burn incinerator. Bulky articles such as mattresses and refrigerators are removed from the garbage to prevent the incinerator from getting clogged. Small pieces of garbage catch fire quickly and burn faster than large chunks of waste. The garbage is moved by conveyor belts into the shredder, which chops it into smaller pieces. It is then burned.

Flyash is poisonous and requires special disposal.

The burning question

Incineration reduces the volume of garbage by 95 percent and also produces some energy. It sounds like the perfect answer to our garbage problem. Unfortunately, incineration does not make garbage disappear. It simply transforms it from one form of waste to another more dangerous form. What begins as solid waste ends up as poisonous ashes and gas.

Dangerous ashes

The two kinds of ashes that remain after incineration are **bottom ash** and **flyash**. Bottom ash is made up of items that did not burn, such as metal, glass, and plastic, plus the ashes of materials that did burn in the incineration process. Flyash refers to the materials that remain after the smoke and gases go through a cleaning process. This is the most dangerous waste created by incineration because it contains various poisons that are harmful to our lives and those of other living beings.

Disposing of the ashes

Around the world bottom ash and flyash have been disposed of in different ways. In some cases they are mixed together and dumped into landfill sites or at the bottom of the ocean. In other cases the flyash is separated and the bottom ash is taken to a landfill site. The flyash is then placed in metal drums and stored in salt caverns or disposed of at hazardous-waste facilities. None of these disposal methods is totally safe. When stored on land, flyash can leach into the ground; when dumped in the ocean, it can poison marine life.

Pollution-control devices

The gases and smoke that pour out of the incinerator's smoke stack are called **pollutants**. Pollutants contain dangerous poisons that threaten our health and cause diseases such as cancer.

Many incineration plants try to control the toxic gas and solids they release into the atmosphere by using pollution-control devices. The smoke and gases from the incinerator pass through these. A **spray cooler** forces the gases through a liquid spray, which cools down the gases and causes some of the pollutants to dissolve in the liquid. The **baghouse**, which consists of a series of fabric filters, collects the solid particles, or flyash, from the gases.

Long-term effects

The newer incinerators are designed to remove most of the poisons from the gases. Scientists are not sure about the long-term effects of these emissions, however, nor have they studied the effects of these gases mixing with other gases, such as those released by various industries. Some countries have not even passed laws requiring the use of pollution-control devices in their incinerators!

(above) Operating an incineration plant is difficult and expensive.

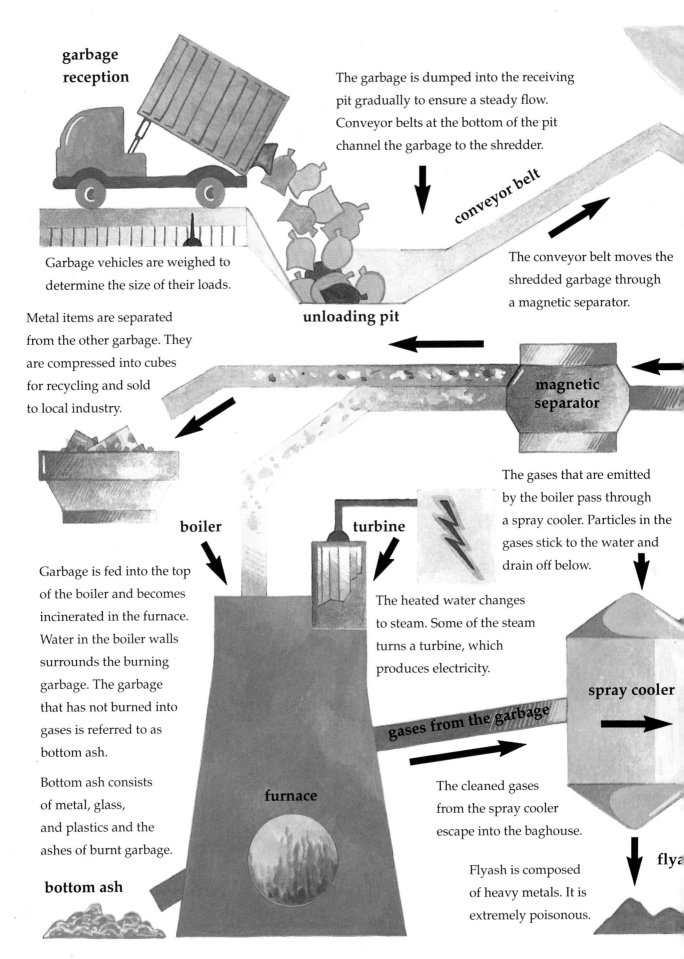

garbage reception

The garbage is dumped into the receiving pit gradually to ensure a steady flow. Conveyor belts at the bottom of the pit channel the garbage to the shredder.

Garbage vehicles are weighed to determine the size of their loads.

unloading pit

conveyor belt

The conveyor belt moves the shredded garbage through a magnetic separator.

Metal items are separated from the other garbage. They are compressed into cubes for recycling and sold to local industry.

magnetic separator

The gases that are emitted by the boiler pass through a spray cooler. Particles in the gases stick to the water and drain off below.

boiler

turbine

The heated water changes to steam. Some of the steam turns a turbine, which produces electricity.

Garbage is fed into the top of the boiler and becomes incinerated in the furnace. Water in the boiler walls surrounds the burning garbage. The garbage that has not burned into gases is referred to as bottom ash.

Bottom ash consists of metal, glass, and plastics and the ashes of burnt garbage.

furnace

gases from the garbage

spray cooler

The cleaned gases from the spray cooler escape into the baghouse.

bottom ash

fly

Flyash is composed of heavy metals. It is extremely poisonous.

When the gases come out of the smoke stack into the atmosphere, they are mostly free of solid particles.

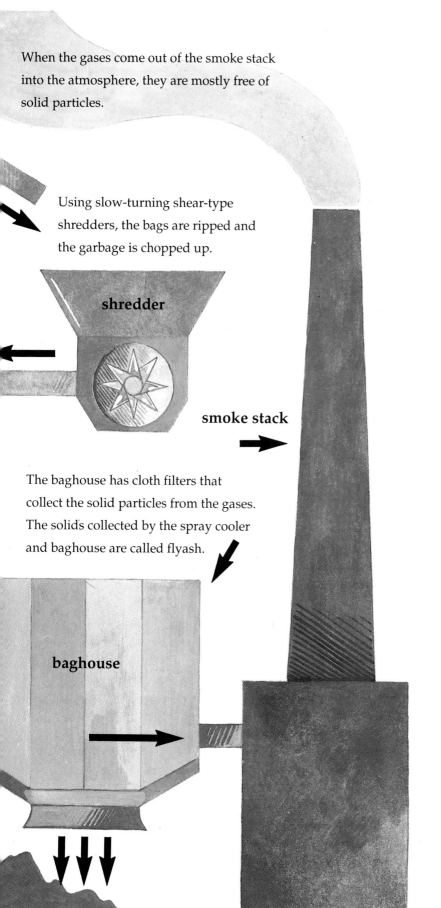

Using slow-turning shear-type shredders, the bags are ripped and the garbage is chopped up.

shredder

smoke stack

The baghouse has cloth filters that collect the solid particles from the gases. The solids collected by the spray cooler and baghouse are called flyash.

baghouse

How incineration works

Energy production

Many incineration companies have described themselves as important energy producers as well as garbage reducers. In an incineration plant the water inside the boiler, where the garbage is burned, changes to steam. The steam turns a turbine that produces electricity. In many cases enough energy is produced to run the incinerator itself and also serve some of the local population's electricity needs. The facts are, however, that incinerators do not use all the energy available in the garbage and that "garbage power" costs much more than electricity that is produced from other energy sources.

Community concerns

Very few people want incineration plants in their communities. They are worried about the fumes, toxic ashes, and the possible accidents that could endanger people's lives. Building and operating an incinerator is also much more expensive than running community recycling and composting programs, which do not pose such serious environmental hazards.

Hazardous wastes in your home

Most people blame business and industry for creating hazardous wastes but, did you know, that some of the most dangerous garbage comes from **your** home? Hazardous wastes don't break down quickly in the environment, and the longer they remain there, the greater the chance for damage to our forests, lakes, streams, wildlife—and also to us.

Many common household articles contain chemicals that can be very harmful to people and the environment. In the last one hundred years modern technology has made it possible for scientists to invent all kinds of chemicals that do not exist in nature. These synthetic chemicals are used in countless ways. They are in paint, cleaning products, fertilizers, and bleach.

Serious health risks

When these chemicals were first introduced, nobody thought it was necessary to test them. Not long afterward, however, people started noticing that some of these chemicals caused cancer and other serious health problems. Today people are more aware of the dangers of poisonous chemicals, but many households still get rid of them in unsafe ways. Toxic chemicals such as leftover paints and thinners, nail polish, batteries, and flammable materials should be taken to hazardous-waste-disposal facilities, where they are stored in special containers and carefully observed.

You can help reduce the dangers posed by hazardous wastes by educating your family about the way they should handle these poisons. Do a household inventory and find out where these products are stored and how your parents have disposed of them in the past. Give them these guidelines to follow in the future:

What you should not do

1. **Don't put hazardous wastes out with your garbage**. They may harm the sanitation workers and cause dangerous leachate and fumes at the landfill site.
2. **Don't bury them**. Toxic substances can contaminate the soil and ground water.
3. **Don't pour hazardous wastes down the drain**. They may corrode plumbing, release toxic fumes, damage sewer systems, and contaminate drinking water.

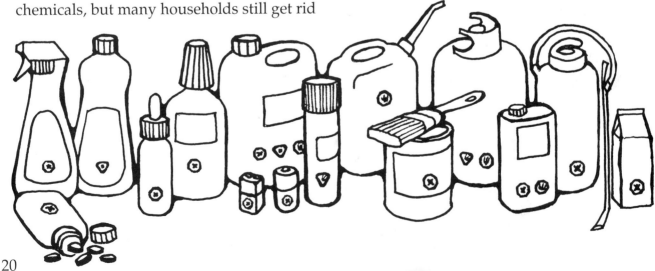

What you should do

- Only buy as much as you need of paints, varnishes, and thinners.
- Store them in a safe place away from heat sources.
- Make sure the containers are sealed.
- When the containers are empty, never use them to store other things. It is important to know what the leftover substances in the containers are in order to dispose of them safely.
- Do not burn, puncture, or crush aerosol cans.
- Exchange or give unwanted paints and chemicals to neighbors who need them.
- Never mix hazardous wastes.
- Dispose of all your hazardous wastes at a special collection site in your community.

If your area has not yet planned a hazardous-waste-disposal program, contact your government officials and persuade them to start one immediately!

Danger signs

You can identify hazardous wastes by the labels on cans and bottles.

Corrosive

Substances such as battery acid and drain cleaners that wear away at many materials

Flammable

Liquids such as lighter fluid and turpentine that can burst into flames

Reactive

Materials that react in dangerous ways when they are mixed with other materials. For example, bleach mixed with ammonia creates deadly fumes.

Toxic

Materials that are poisonous to you and your pets, even in small quantities. Rat poison, some medicines, cleaning fluids, pesticides, and bleach are examples.

Using substitutes

Instead of using dangerous products in your home, persuade your parents to use safe substitutes. Many people know of at least one or two alternative cleaning substances that can be used in place of toxic chemicals. For example, salt, vinegar, and baking soda work well for a variety of cleaning jobs. Using substitutes is not only safer for the environment, but it means that you do not have to buy and then dispose of toxic substances.

Salt, vinegar, and baking soda can tackle many household cleaning jobs.

Our garbage stream

Where does your garbage go? Trace the path it takes after you separate it at home.

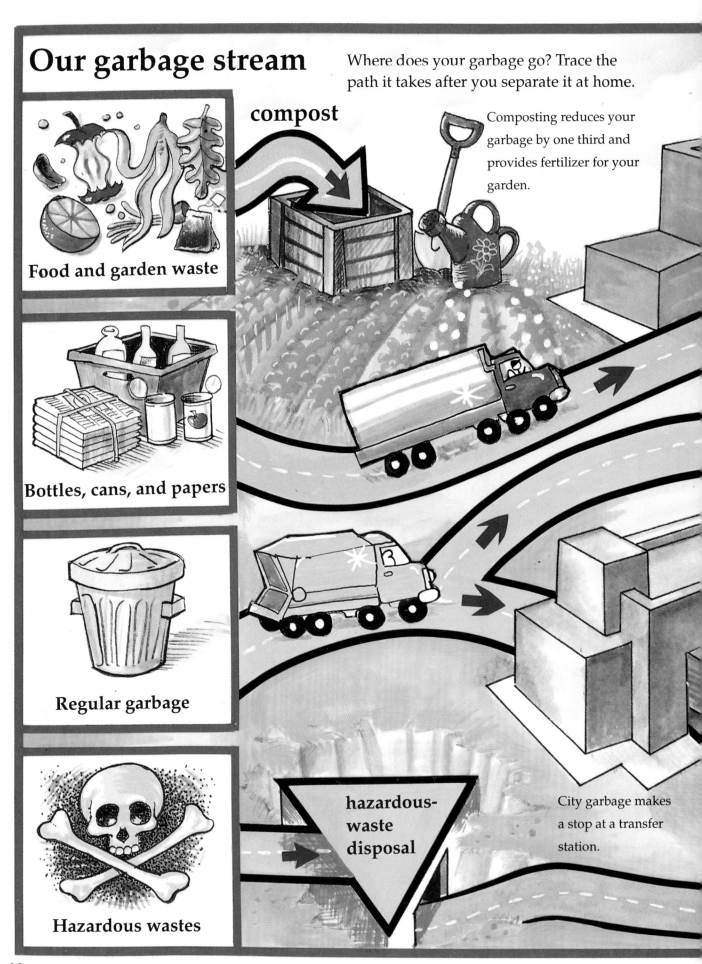

compost

Composting reduces your garbage by one third and provides fertilizer for your garden.

Food and garden waste

Bottles, cans, and papers

Regular garbage

Hazardous wastes

hazardous-waste disposal

City garbage makes a stop at a transfer station.

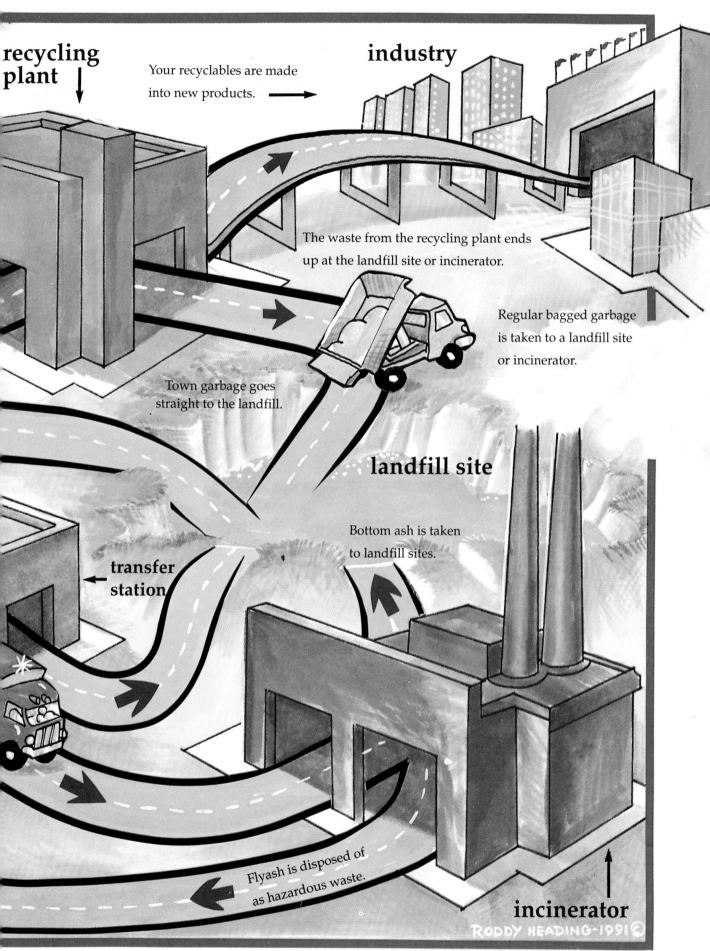

recycling plant

industry

Your recyclables are made into new products. →

The waste from the recycling plant ends up at the landfill site or incinerator.

Regular bagged garbage is taken to a landfill site or incinerator.

Town garbage goes straight to the landfill.

landfill site

Bottom ash is taken to landfill sites.

transfer station

Flyash is disposed of as hazardous waste.

incinerator

RODDY HEADING·1991©

More than just three Rs

We now know that landfilling and incineration are not good solutions to our garbage crisis, but what positive steps can we take to get rid of our trash? There are ways that each one of us can make a difference in cleaning up our world, but these require self-discipline and sacrifice. We must learn to do without things that we do not need, and we need to take time to think about ways to cut down on the things we throw away.

The following are good methods of dealing with our garbage crisis. Most of you have heard about reduction, reuse, and recycling. We have added a few more ways to help you cut down on your garbage.

Reducing garbage

By far, reduction is the most important way of managing our waste. Reducing waste means cutting down on the garbage we would normally throw away. Reusing, recycling, and composting all have one aim—to reduce our garbage.

The greatest challenge in reducing our garbage is getting into the habit of purchasing less. We should avoid buying things we really do not need. By reducing what we buy, we also reduce the amount of garbage we have to throw out.

Refusing

One way to reduce our purchases is to say no to products that create unnecessary garbage. For example, refusing to buy fad items means not having to throw them away and replace them with new fad items. We can also refuse to buy products that are harmful to the environment. We can refuse to waste food, paper, and clothes. And most important of all, we can refuse to buy disposable and convenience items!

Reusing

Reusing means saving items that would otherwise be thrown out and using them over again. For instance, giving your magazines to a dentist's waiting room or buying goods at a garage sale are both reusing activities. Reusing results in reducing garbage because we are cutting down on the amount we buy and discard.

Samantha and Barney take one last look at the magazines before they give them away.

A mountain of cans for recycling!

Recycling

Many items such as cans and newspapers cannot be reused directly, but they can be saved from the useless garbage heap by being recycled. Since garbage came from valuable natural resources, it makes sense not to waste them. Recycling allows us to recover some of these natural resources and turn them into new products. Recycling is another great way to reduce our garbage and save our remaining resources.

Don't just recycle, precycle

Precycling is choosing products packaged in refillable and recyclable materials. You precycle before you buy, and recycle the packaging afterwards. You can precycle by:

- buying milk in refillable jugs
- buying soft drinks in returnable bottles
- buying eggs in cardboard boxes
- buying food in recyclable cans or jars
- looking for "recycled" logos on boxes
- choosing unwrapped items when possible

Rebuying

Recycling programs have caught on extremely well in almost every community. People want to know what they can do to help, and recycling requires very little effort. Unfortunately, many people do not realize that putting cans, bottles, and newspapers into their blue boxes is only **source separation**, the first step in the recycling process. They are not completing the recycling cycle to make it all work.

At the present time, relatively few companies produce goods made from recycled materials. The result is that a lot of cans, bottles, and newspapers are piling up in large recycling warehouses because there is not enough demand for them. You can help by "rebuying" goods made from recycled materials. The more recycled goods you buy, the sooner manufacturers will make more recycled products.

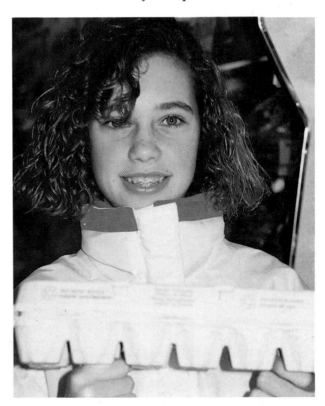

Cardboard egg boxes are recycled and break down much faster at a landfill than Styrofoam ones.

Composting—the natural way

humus

All living things produce waste products, either through their digestive systems or when they die and return to the earth. Nature's way of disposing of waste is called **decomposition**. Small organisms called bacteria cause materials to decompose, or rot. As a result, everything eventually breaks down into simpler parts, which are used again in nature's never-ending cycle of life. Some substances break down faster than others. Most food items rot quickly.

Separating your biodegradables

One simple way of reducing your garbage is by using the power of nature to get rid of it for you. You can cut down on one third of your garbage by starting a compost. **Composting** is the separation of food wastes and other biodegradable materials from household garbage so they can disintegrate naturally. Biodegradable items break down within a short time.

In a compost heap, vegetable and garden waste is piled together and left to rot. Over time it decomposes into a rich, black, soil-like material called **humus**. Humus is good for the environment because, when it is added to your garden as a fertilizer, it provides essential nutrients to the soil.

Composting is a way of using the three Rs. You **reduce** the amount of garbage that goes to the landfill, you **recycle** biodegradable materials to make fertilizer, and you **reuse** the garbage, which is changed to humus, to grow new fruits and vegetables. Composting also helps eliminate the use of chemical fertilizers on your lawn or garden.

Biodegradables are changed to rich, black humus.

How to compost

Since composting is part of nature's cycle, it is really quite simple to do. You can either buy or make a composting bin or dig a pit into which you place your composting materials. Collect all your kitchen scraps such as fruit and vegetable peels, egg shells, tea leaves, and coffee grounds in a sealed container. When the container is full, dump its contents into your composter along with any yard waste such as leaves and grass clippings. Meat, bones, and fatty foods should not be composted because they create odors and attract animals.

Once in a while you might want to throw in a few handfuls of soil or some earthworms to help your compost decompose. As your kitchen scraps rot, the compost heap will start to "cook," or warm up a bit. This is part of the natural process of decomposition.

Community composting

One way a community could cut down on the amount of rubbish it sends to the landfill is by setting up a "municipal solid-waste composting site." Some communities are already involved in this type of large-scale composting, as shown in the photographs on this page. Their garbage is taken to a composting site instead of a landfill. Although municipal composting sites are still few, many communities have started to encourage composting—even in apartment buildings.

Encourage composting

Composting is a natural, simple way to reduce trash. It is one of the best ways to cut down on garbage. You can make a big difference to the environment by encouraging composting. Convince as many people as you can to start now!

Regular "green-bag garbage" is brought to this municipal solid-waste composting site.

Pickers take out hazardous materials and large objects from unsorted garbage.

The remaining garbage is ground up small and left indoors in a composting area, where it decomposes for about a month. After it is ground one more time and sifted, it is moved outdoors where the piles cool down. Weeks later the compost is ready to be sold as a natural fertilizer.

Do you know...?

... that packaging is instant garbage?

Packaging makes up more than one third of our garbage. Not only is it garbage, it is **instant** garbage. It has no value once the product it contains is removed. The harm packaging causes the environment does not just happen at the landfill or incinerator. It starts when the packaging is created. Before you reach for that next attractive box on your store shelf, consider these problems caused by packaging:

- Valuable natural resources such as trees and petroleum are used to create cardboard, plastic, and polystyrene foam, which make up most packaging materials.
- When these natural resources are processed or made into cardboard, plastic, and polystyrene foam, toxic chemicals are released into the environment.
- The factories that make boxes, trays, and cartons from these materials release more toxic wastes into the air and water.
- Transporting the packages by truck to the factories, stores, and then to the landfill site produces yet more air pollution.
- When plastic packaging is incinerated, toxic fumes are again released into the air.
- At the landfill site, when the packaging breaks down, poisonous leachate seeps into the ground water.
- Excess packaging hurts people in other parts of the world, too. We are now using up the natural resources found in third-world countries as we are running out of resources in the industrialized parts of the world.

... that white products are dangerous?

White products such as writing paper, facial tissues, toilet paper, paper towels, napkins, and milk cartons have been bleached of their natural color. When paper products are bleached, large amounts of poisonous chemical wastes are dumped into the waterways. These chemicals are not just in the waste! They can also be found in the paper products you use. By buying bleached paper products, you may be eating and drinking unwanted chemicals!

You can help eliminate the use of bleach by not buying white paper products. Almost every supermarket now carries recycled paper products, which are beige. Even better, you can cut down on your use of paper products altogether by using rags instead of paper towels and cloth napkins instead of paper ones.

Most supermarkets now carry recycled paper products, which have not been bleached.

... why you should avoid Styrofoam?

Polystyrene foam, better known as Styrofoam, is used to make cups, food containers, plates, packaging inserts, and egg cartons. All these things are meant to be thrown away as soon as they are used. Here are just a few reasons why you should avoid using Styrofoam.

- Styrofoam is non-biodegradable. It stays around in its original form for hundreds and even thousands of years. It is permanent garbage!
- When Styrofoam is swallowed by animals or fish, it can cause death.
- Styrofoam contains a large amount of air, so it takes up a lot of landfill space.
- Polystyrene foam is made using products that are harmful to the **ozone layer**, the layer of our atmosphere that protects us from the dangerous rays of the sun.

You can help reduce the use of Styrofoam by not buying cups and plates made from it and by avoiding products that are packaged in it.

... the facts about disposable diapers?

Do you know a baby who wears disposable diapers? Perhaps you can persuade his or her parents to switch to cloth diapers once you give them all the facts:

- A baby uses 10,000 diapers by the time he or she is toilet trained.
- Disposable diapers can take 500 years to decompose in a landfill site.
- A very large portion of the earth's natural resources go into creating the pulp and plastic needed to make the diapers.
- Disposable diapers are bleached white and contain dangerous particles of dioxin,

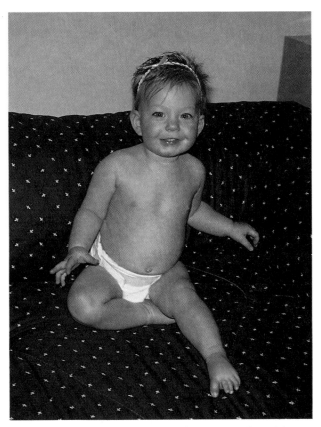

Cloth diapers are healthier and more comfortable for a baby and better for the environment. Kirsten feels much happier wearing them!

which attach themselves to the oils in a baby's skin. They may be absorbed into the baby's bloodstream.

- Although manufacturers of disposable diapers suggest that the diapers be rinsed before they are thrown out, very few parents follow these directions. Human waste is meant to end up at a sewage-treatment plant where it can be properly treated. Untreated human waste, which carries bacteria and viruses, should not be disposed of at a landfill.
- Cloth diapers are not made from trees; they are made from cotton plants, which are easy to grow. When cotton diapers eventually end up in a landfill, they disintegrate in only six months. Using cloth diapers is a better alternative both for the baby and the environment!

Your personal action plan

Do you have your own personal action plan?

In order to cut down on your garbage, you must make a committment. You need to adopt a new attitude about the environment and then take the responsibility for cleaning it up. You can help by writing down some goals and then doing something every single day. Sample goals might be:

- Reducing your "wants" and not buying things that you do not really need
- Trading what you have with others instead of buying new things
- Not buying disposable and convenience items
- Recycling cans, bottles, and papers
- Buying recycled products whenever possible
- Avoiding products that are harmful to the environment and using safe substitutes
- Composting your food scraps

- Buying as much as possible without packaging and avoiding fancy packages
- Bringing your lunch in reusable containers and using cloth napkins
- Becoming informed about environmental issues and informing others
- Becoming conscious of everything you throw away and setting a goal to reduce your garbage a little each week
- Keeping a diary of everything you did to reduce your garbage each day

Using your daily diary, you can calculate how much you have reused, reduced, and recycled in a month. You can also keep track of the long-term ecology projects you have started or accomplished. How did these accomplishments make you feel? Give yourself a big pat on the back for all your hard work!

Glossary

baghouse A filtering system that removes solid particles from gases during incineration

biodegradable A substance capable of breaking down into a harmless form

boiler An enclosed vessel in which burning garbage heats water for making electricity

bottom ash Items that did not burn during incineration, such as glass and plastic, plus the ashes of burnt materials

compost A mixture of vegetable matter and other biodegradables that break down into fertilizer over a relatively short period of time

consumer society A society that uses articles made by others

contamination The process of becoming infected or diseased

convenience item A prepared and packaged item

decompose To rot or disintegrate

dioxin A poisonous substance produced in many manufacturing processes

disposable Something that can be thrown away

durability The ability to resist wear, decay, or change

ecology The study of the relationship between living things and their environment

environment The surroundings that affect the existence of living beings

flyash The highly poisonous materials that remain after the smoke and gases pass through the filters in an incinerator

ground water Water that is beneath the earth

hazardous waste Garbage that is dangerous to living beings

landfill site A place where garbage is buried under and on top of layers of dirt

leachate Poisonous materials that pollute water as it seeps through solid waste

magnetic separator A piece of machinery that uses the power of a magnet to separate certain types of metals from other types

methane A colorless, odorless, highly flammable gas created by decaying organic matter

monitor To check or watch

natural resources Materials found in nature that are useful to people or necessary to their survival, such as water, trees, and minerals

ozone layer A layer of gas that purifies the air and protects living beings from the harmful rays of the sun

packaging A wrapping or container into which something is packed

pollutant Waste that pollutes air, water, or soil

polystyrene foam A lightweight plastic used in making drinking cups, etc. Commonly known as Styrofoam

processed Made or prepared by some special method

pulp A soft, moist, formless mass, such as the mixture of matted fibers of wood that is used in making paper

refuse Waste, rubbish

spray cooler A system that cools down gas emissions in an incinerator before they are filtered

synthetic Not made from natural materials

third world Describing countries that are considered less developed in their industry and social programs

toxic waste Poisonous garbage

transfer station A place where city garbage is taken to be sorted and compacted

turbine A machine that turns steam or flowing water into electric power

Index & Acknowledgements

Special thanks to: DeLaat's Valumart, Tricil Limited, Agripost, EarthSource, and "Garbage" magazine.
Photo Credits: Courtesy of Agripost, Pompano Beach, Florida: 27; Peter Crabtree & Bobbie Kalman: 4, 5, 6 (top and bottom left), 9, 21, 24, 25, 28, 29, 30; Marc Crabtree: 8; Ontario Archives: (S 5695); Courtesy of the Ontario Ministry of the Environment: Cover and title page, 6 (bottom right), 11, 13, 15, 16, 17. **Artwork:** Michael Turner: 12, 18-19, 26; David Willis: 20, 21; Roddy Heading: 22-23

3 4 5 6 7 8 9 Printed in U.S.A. 0 9 8 7 6 5 4 3